The Relational God

A 10-Session, Printable PDF Bible Study

What the Bible Says about Our Identities As:
Sons and Daughters
Husbands and Wives
Brothers and Sisters
Fathers and Mothers
How Those Relationships Thrive
and What They Teach Us about God

Steven J. Halbert

The Relational God Bible Study: What the Bible Says about Our Identities as Sons and Daughters, Husbands and Wives, Brothers and Sisters, Fathers and Mothers—How Those Relationships Thrive and What They Teach Us about God

Copyright © 2020 by Steven J. Halbert

Published by Tusitala Publishers, 206 Sassafras Drive; Taylors, SC 29687

All rights reserved. No part of this publication may be reproduced without the prior permission of the publisher, except as provided for by US copyright law.

Cover design: Steven J. Halbert
Cover image: Aunt Kitty

Edited by: Steven J. Halbert

Fillable PDF by: Steven J. Halbert

Printed in the United States of America, First Printing 2020

Scripture quotations, unless otherwise noted, are from ESV® Bible (The Holy Bible, English Standard Version®), copyright © 2001, 2007, 2011, 2016 by Crossway, a publishing ministry of Good News Publishers. Used by permission. All rights reserved. Scripture marked KJV is taken from the King James Version of the Bible. Scripture quotations marked NIV are taken from the Holy Bible, New International Version®, NIV® Copyright ©1973, 1978, 1984, 2011 by Biblica, Inc.® Used by permission. All rights reserved worldwide. Scripture quotations marked (NASB) taken from the New American Standard Bible® (NASB), Copyright © 1960, 1962, 1963, 1968, 1971, 1972, 1973, 1975, 1977, 1995 by The Lockman Foundation Used by permission. www.Lockman.org.

Trade paperback ISBN: 978-0-9993099-6-4
Printable PDF ISBN: 978-0-9993099-7-1
Fillable PDF ISBN: 978-1-7343882-5-1

Library of Congress Cataloging-in-Publication Data

Names: Halbert, Steven Joseph, 1983- author.
Title: The Relational God Bible Study: What the Bible Says about Our Identities as Sons and Daughters, Husbands and Wives, Brothers and Sisters, Fathers and Mothers–How Those Relationships Thrive and What They Teach Us about God
Description: Greenville: Tusitala Publishers, 2020.
Library of Congress Control Number: 2019904660

An Introductory Letter from the Author

Writing this book and Bible study has been one of the greatest challenges of my life. God has used this study to convict me in my relationships as a son, a husband, a brother, and a father. By no stretch of the imagination have I "arrived."

Indeed, one of the very reasons I began searching the Bible for these relationships was to understand better what God's word says to us as children, spouses, siblings, and parents.

Mostly, because I needed to know. I needed for these relationships to be better.

So why are *you* here?

What are *you* hoping to gain from this study?

> **WHERE YOU HAVE PROBLEMS INTERPERSONALLY, YOU MAY DISCOVER THOSE SAME TENDENCIES AS THORNY AREAS SPIRITUALLY.**

This study can help you identify the roots of those issues. Since relationships are dynamic, this may be a resource you return to again-and-again as your identity in one or more of these relationships shifts.

Whatever the case, this study is meant to be viewed and re-viewed. The Holy Spirit has certainly used it in my own life to reveal sinful tendencies I didn't even know I had.

Family can be difficult, so this study may challenge you in very emotional ways. I would encourage you to stick with it, even if the going gets tough.

> **LEAN ON YOUR BROTHERS AND SISTERS IN CHRIST.**
>
> **OPEN UP TO THEM.**
>
> **BE TRANSPARENT.**

Since our relationships are among the most sensitive topics we can discuss, it is my prayer that the discussions that occur as a result of this study will be marked with grace. Our relational experiences are vast and far reaching, so it is important that we are biblical in our approach. And part of being biblical also means being gentle with one another and treating one another with kindness and Christlike love.

As our familial relationships thrive, they will reflect something about the nature and character of God Himself. This is how He designed it. Our relationships are metaphors. When they thrive, they point to the one who made them. The rewards are both temporal and eternal.

PUT IN THE TIME.

PRAY FOR WISDOM.

ACT WITH BOLDNESS AND COURAGE.

YOU'LL BE GLAD YOU DID.

It is my sincere prayer that God will use this study in your life to strengthen your relationships with your immediate family members, your relationships with your brothers and sisters in Christ, and, ultimately, your relationship with God.

Grace and Peace,

Steven J. Halbert

--Steven J. Halbert

P.S. I would like to offer a HUGE shout-out and special thanks to the following groups: the Sunday school class led by Dustin Manwaring at Simpsonville First Baptist Church in Simpsonville, SC; the Life Group led by Russ Nuss at Life Springs Church in Zebulon, GA; and the Sunday night GROW class at Edwards Road Baptist Church in Greenville, SC for test-driving this curriculum and offering invaluable feedback. The study is *much* better because of your involvement and suggestions. Thank you!

Table of Contents

An Introductory Letter from the Author iii

Table of Contents v

Session 1 - Introduction 1

Session 2 - Children: How to Be a Child 9

Session 3 - Children Sons and Daughters of God 17

Session 4 - Marriage: How to Be a Spouse I 23

Session 5 - Marriage: How to Be a Spouse II 37

Session 6 - Marriage: Christ and the Church 51

Session 7 - Siblings: How to Be a Sibling 59

Session 8 - Parents: How to Be a Parent 69

Session 9 - Parents: The Mother and Father Heart of God 79

Session 10 - Adoption: A New Forever Family 87

A Concluding Letter from the Author 95

Appendix A - Book: Intro through Chapter 2 97

Therefore be imitators of God, as beloved children. And walk in love, as Christ loved us and gave himself up for us, a fragrant offering and sacrifice to God.

Ephesians 5:1–2

Session 1 - Introduction

Format

The Broad Overview

The Relational God Bible study is a 10-session study designed to explore the biblical command for our identities as sons and daughters, husbands and wives, brothers and sisters, and mothers and fathers. The course will then examine the practical spiritual implications of those commands.

The 10-sessions are divided into the following *sections*:

- Introduction and Overview
- Child – 2x (Physically Practical and Spiritually Practical)
- Spouse – 3x (Physically Practical and Spiritually Practical)
- Sibling – 1x (Physically Practical and Spiritually Practical)
- Parent – 2x (Physically Practical and Spiritually Practical)
- Adoption and Conclusion

Each relationship section will also have an *optional* "Service" component with suggestions for how you can work out the concepts you are learning during that portion of the study; however, I encourage you to consider getting involved with complimentary programs at your local church before tackling something brand new.

Session-by-Session

The Bible study is designed to facilitate discussion and application of the material from the companion book (*The Relational God*) in your life (either in a group setting or individually). Thus, each session is arranged like this:

- **Big Idea** – the main theme of the session
- **Key Scripture** – the primary Scripture(s) to be reviewed for that session
- **Read** – the corresponding chapter(s) to read prior to the group session (the first two chapters are included in Appendix A of the study)
- **Key Concepts** – questions to answer while you read
- **Community Study and Discussion** – material to facilitate discussion and application of the key concepts

Additional Guidance

The final page(s) of each session are blank for you to sketch, doodle, or take additional notes (however best facilitates comprehension and application in your own life).

There is a Leader's Guide available for individuals wishing to teach and/or facilitate the contents of this study. So, in addition to the previous bullets, there may be a Teaching component as well. In this case, you may or may not do the reading, so you will look for the answers to the "Key Concept" portion during the teaching.

For sessions when you are left with extra time, I would encourage you to use that time judiciously. Pray for one another. Take time to plan a service project. Fellowship. Build community!

The Goal

Ultimately, **the goal of this study is to understand what the Bible says about how to improve your relationships with your family, with the body of Christ, and with your own personal walk with the Lord.** With that goal in mind, is there really anything more important you could be pursuing? I ask that, because any time you begin something new, you make a mental determination about the priority you will give to it. I urge you to take this study seriously. It may mean giving up a couple lunch breaks at work each week. It may mean having a conversation with your family about getting out of the house for an hour or two, so you can focus on your spiritual growth. It may mean being more vulnerable with your brothers and sisters in Christ than you are used to. Speaking up more. Sharing more of your life. Whatever it means for you, I can promise that the time you spend searching God's Word and opening up to your brothers and sisters in Christ will yield value in your life, as Paul reminds us:

> RATHER, TRAIN YOURSELF FOR GODLINESS; FOR WHILE BODILY TRAINING IS OF SOME VALUE, GODLINESS IS OF VALUE IN EVERY WAY, AS IT HOLDS PROMISE FOR THE PRESENT LIFE AND ALSO FOR THE LIFE TO COME. THE SAYING IS TRUSTWORTHY AND DESERVING OF FULL ACCEPTANCE. FOR TO THIS END WE TOIL AND STRIVE, BECAUSE WE HAVE OUR HOPE SET ON THE LIVING GOD, WHO IS THE SAVIOR OF ALL PEOPLE, ESPECIALLY OF THOSE WHO BELIEVE. (1 TIMOTHY 4:7–10)

Themes and References

The tables below contain a framework from which to consider the themes and Scripture we will study during this course. It's a good summary and provides a roadmap for the course.

THEMES			
	Biblical Commands	Us to God	God
Child	• Honor • Obey • Learn	• Shifting Dependence • Spiritual Maturity • We Are God's Children	• Jesus as the Son of God
Spouse	• Wives–Submit • Husbands–Love • Leave and Hold Fast • Physical Intimacy • Faithfulness • Misc. Commands	• Christ and the Church • The Spiritual Covenant	• The Godhead
Sibling	• Warnings • Unity • Greeting • Support/Prayer • Equity	• Bros. & Sis. w/Christ (vertical) • Bros. & Sis. In Christ (horizontal)	• Jesus the Firstborn among Many Brothers
Parent	• Teach/Model • Discipline • Gentleness • Love	• Spiritual Parenting • Teaching & Modeling • Discipline • Prayer & Generosity	• God as father • Mother Heart of God • Jesus as Son of God

REFERENCES			
	Biblical Commands	Us to God	God
Child	• Exodus 20:12 • Luke 2:41–52 • Ephesians 6:1–3	• Romans 8:14–17, 29 • Galatians 3:15–4:7 • Hebrews 5:12–14; 12:3–11 • 1 John 2:12–14	• John 1:1–4, 14 • John 3:14–17
Spouse	• 1 Corinthians 7 • Ephesians 5:15–33 • Colossians 3:19 • 1 Peter 3:7 • Titus 2:3–5	• Luke 14:26 • Romans 12:4–8 • 1 Corinthians 12 • Ephesians 5:22–32 • Revelation 19:6–9; 21:4, 9–11	• John 15:1–17 • Romans 7:1–6 • Colossians 1:15–20
Sibling	• Matthew 5:22–24; 7:3–5 • Romans 1:11–13; 15:25–30; 16:14 • 2 Thessalonians 3:15 • 1 John 2:9–11; 3:10–16; 4:20–21	• Mark 10:29–30 • Romans 8:14–17, 29 • Hebrews 2:5–3:6	• N/A
Parent	• Deuteronomy 6:4–9 • Proverbs 13:24; 19:18 • Ephesians 6:4 • Titus 2:4	• Matthew 7:7–11; 28:19 • John 15:12–16 • Romans 8:15 • Hebrews 12:5–10	• John 15:12–16 • Colossians 1:15 • Titus 3:3–7 • James 3:17–18

And let us consider how we may spur one another on toward love and good deeds

Hebrews 10:24 (NIV)

Community Study and Discussion

Each session, the Bible study will begin with questions designed to foster discussion and share experiences. As I've already said, don't be afraid to open-up and share with your brothers and sisters. By so doing, you will "spur one another on toward love and good deeds" (Hebrews 10:24, NIV).

So, even though this is just an introduction session, here are the questions to get you started with the study. Feel free to work through these questions however you think best for the group (together as a whole group, breaking into smaller groups, etc.).

What are the four physical relationships specifically established by God [hint: look at cover page]?

God could have made us to be in any sort of relationships. Why those?

Of the God-given relationships (the relationships specifically established by God), which do you think could use the most work in your life? Why?

Now think about each of those four relationships on the title page. What is at least one thing you would like to see improved in each of those relationships? If you do not have one or more of those relationships, think about it spiritually for a moment. What would you like to see improved in that area spiritually?

What else are you hoping to get out of this study (why are you here)?

Final page(s) for sketching, doodling, or additional thoughts / notes

Session 2 – Children: How to Be a Child

Personal Study

Big Idea

CHILDREN ARE TO HONOR, OBEY, AND LEARN FROM THEIR PARENTS; AND THE GOAL OF CHILDHOOD IS TO SHIFT DEPENDENCE FROM OUR PARENTS AND ON TO _____.

Key Scripture

EXODUS 20:12 | LUKE 2:41–52 | EPHESIANS 6:1–3

Read

CHAPTERS 1 AND 2 OF *THE RELATIONAL GOD*

Key Concepts (look for the answers to these questions while you read):

What does it mean to honor?

_____

_____

_____

When can we stop obeying our parents?

_____

_____

_____

What is the goal of childhood?

How does Jesus model the goal of childhood?

How are we to learn?

Community Study and Discussion

In your current season of life, what do you find most difficult about honoring your parents? If your parents are no longer living, is there a way in which you could honor the memory of your parent(s)? Would you be willing to share things that you wish you had done to honor your parents while they were still alive?

Is there anything additional that you could do *this week* to honor your parents, honor their memory, or share your experience with others?

Another primary role of a child is to learn, what are some lessons that you learned from you parents (positive and negative)?

What else could your parents still teach you? If your parents are alive, could you go to them for advice or honor them by spending time with them and listening to their story?

The reading identified two types of learning (life lessons and the development of new skill sets). You are in this class, so you are at least actively involved in learning (great work). What else might the Lord want you to learn?

Finally, the reading emphasized the goal of childhood as *shifting dependence*. **In what areas are you not depending fully on the Lord? What could you relinquish to Him** *this week* **?**

If the commands to us as physical children are to honor, obey, and learn from our parents, how do you think these same commands translate spiritually (as we are the children of God)?

Honor your father and your mother, that your days may be long in the land that the **Lord** your God is giving you.

Exodus 20:12

Service

Be thinking about how your group can serve children. There are *a lot* of ways to serve children. Brainstorm as a group about how you might serve the children in your community. Ask your pastor(s) about current church programs that serve children. Are there any needs that your group can help meet over the next two sessions (or longer)? Here are some ideas to get you started (perhaps nominate an individual to coordinate):

- Consider partnering with a local ministry that ministers to children.
- Consider partnering with a national or international ministry to support a child in another country.
- Children in foster care are some of the most vulnerable in our society. How can your group bless a child in foster care (or an agency which works with foster children)?
- How can you help disciple the children in your church towards spiritual maturity?
- As we have seen, one command to which most of the participants in this study are not actually beholden is obedience. Are there creative and loving ways that your group can help parents in the church encourage the children within the church towards obedience to their parents?

Other Ideas, Notes, Organization

Final page(s) for sketching, doodling, or additional thoughts / notes

Session 3 - Children Sons and Daughters of God

Personal Study

Big Idea

WE ARE SONS AND DAUGHTERS OF GOD (THROUGH CHRIST); THEREFORE, WE NEED TO GROW UP IN THE LORD.

Key Scripture

JOHN 1:1–4, 14; 3:14–17; 15:1–17 | ROMANS 8:14–17
GALATIANS 3:15–4:7 | 1 JOHN 2:12–14

Read

CHAPTER 3 OF *THE RELATIONAL GOD*

Key Concepts (look for the answers to these questions while you read):

What is the role of Christ when thinking about our position as children of God?

How do we become children of God? Have you done that? If not, are you open to it?

What are the different stages of spiritual development in the life of the believer? What characterizes each?

What is at the root of the word for *discipline*? What about *train*?

Community Study and Discussion

Read 1 John 2:12–14 and identify the four stages of spiritual development in your own words:

Now circle which stage you most identify with.

Little children, what are your current struggles? How could the group help you in those struggles?

Children, what are your current struggles? How could the group help you in those struggles?

Youth, what are your current struggles? How could the group help you in those struggles?

Parents, what are your current struggles? How could the group help you in those struggles?

What are some things you can do *this week* to move forward in your spiritual development? What are some things that might take longer than a week that you can do to move forward in your spiritual development?

During last session's Community Study, you recorded some things that you could do to honor your parents. How's that going? What are some steps you still need to take to make that happen?

How do the physical commands that we examined for children (obey, honor, and learn) affect our understanding of how we grow up spiritually in the Lord?

If Jesus is the Son of God and we are the sons and daughters of God through Jesus, how is Jesus different than us? Read Romans 8:14–17; Galatians 3:15–4:7; and John 1:1–4, 14 as you think about your answer.

Final page(s) for sketching, doodling, or additional thoughts / notes

Session 4 - Marriage: How to Be a Spouse 1

Personal Study

Big Idea

IN BIBLICAL MARRIAGE, BOTH SPOUSES ARE CALLED TO PHYSICAL INTIMACY AND FAITHFULNESS. HUSBANDS SPECIFICALLY ARE CALLED TO LOVE THEIR WIVES; LEAVE CHILDHOOD; AND LIVE WITH THEIR WIVES IN GENTLENESS, UNDERSTANDING, AND HONOR. WIVES SPECIFICALLY ARE CALLED TO LOVE AND SUBMIT TO THEIR HUSBANDS, BE SELF-CONTROLLED, PURE, KIND, AND KEEP THE HOME.

Key Scripture

1 CORINTHIANS 13:4–7 | EPHESIANS 5:15–33

Read

CHAPTERS 4 AND 5 OF *THE RELATIONAL GOD*

Key Concepts (look for the answers to these questions while you read):

What is the context for the commands to spouses in Ephesians?

What is the primary command in Ephesians for wives?

What is the difference between "submission" (*hupotassō*) and "obedience" (*hupakouō*)?

What are the primary commands in Ephesians for husbands?

In the created order, why might these commands be in place?

Whose role should I be concerned with in my marriage?

> HUSBANDS, LOVE YOUR WIVES, AS CHRIST LOVED THE CHURCH AND GAVE HIMSELF UP FOR HER . . .
>
> Ephesians 5:22

Community Study and Discussion (men)

For this Community Study and Discussion, it might be best to split into groups of men and women if there are individuals who are willing to facilitate discussion.

At this point, we need to recognize that the body of Christ is diverse. Some of the individuals taking this study may be in a great marriage. Some marriages may be falling apart. Some may be divorced. Some may be single. That is okay. I would encourage you to not let your status keep you from the truths in God's Word, because, remember, there is a purpose to studying the commands in Scripture for these relationships. Through these commands we can understand something about the nature and character of God. So, again, open-up and share with one another. Don't be afraid to learn from one another's experiences, both good and bad.

What are your thoughts about how you're doing as a husband after this past session's reading?

_____

_____

Let's review some of the concepts as we think about how to be more biblical husbands. Read Ephesians 5 (so you understand context) and answer the following questions.

What is the specific call to husbands (vv. 25–30)?

_____

_____

_____

_____

_____

What are some practical ways that you can focus on loving your wife as vv. 25–30 describe? [what are you doing well that you should keep doing? upon what could you improve?] [list some practical steps to help you improve (both this week and into the future)]

_____

_____

_____

_____

I am repeating the exercise at the end of chapter 5 here, because I think it is very helpful. Read 1 Corinthians 13:4–7 and replace "love" with your name:

_____ is patient and kind;

_____ does not envy or boast;

_____ is not arrogant or rude.

_____ does not insist on [his] own way;

_____ is not irritable or resentful;

_____ does not rejoice at wrongdoing, but rejoices with the truth.

_____ bears all things, believes all things, hopes all things, endures all things. (1 Corinthians 13:4–7)

Which of these is most true? Which is least true? Share them with your wife. Which does she think is most true and least true? How can you work on this?

_____

_____

_____

_____

What could you do this week to serve your spouse. Is it possible to do this unconditionally (i.e. if she doesn't notice or say "thank you," can you be content that you did this for the glory of God)? How could the group encourage you in this?

How might what you are learning about the scriptural commands for marriage be applicable to how our marriages reflect the relationship between Christ and the church?

During last session's Community Study and Discussion, you recorded how the group could help you on your journey towards spiritual maturity. Where have you struggled this week and where have you found success in your journey towards spiritual maturity? How could your community encourage you on the next steps?

> ## WIVES, SUBMIT TO YOUR OWN HUSBANDS, AS TO THE LORD
>
> Ephesians 5:22

Community Study and Discussion (women)

For this Community Study and Discussion, it might be best to split into groups of men and women if there are individuals who are willing to facilitate discussion.

At this point, we need to recognize that the body of Christ is diverse. Some of the individuals taking this study may be in a great marriage. Some marriages may be falling apart. Some may be divorced. Some may be single. That is okay. I would encourage you to not let your status keep you from the truths in God's Word, because, remember, there is a purpose to studying the commands in Scripture for these relationships. Through these commands we can understand something about the nature and character of God. So, again, open-up and share with one another. Don't be afraid to learn from one another's experiences, both good and bad.

What are your thoughts about how you're doing as a wife after this past session's reading?

Let's review some of the concepts as we think about how to be more biblical wives. Read Ephesians 5 (so you understand context) and answer the following questions.

What is the specific call to wives (vv. 22–24)?

How does the church submit to Christ? Start in the same letter (Ephesians) to think about this. Look at Ephesians 1:22. It is interesting to note that this same word (*hupotassō*) is used about Christ in this verse. Now look at Ephesians chapter 4's discussion of Christ as the head of the church. How does that influence your reading of Ephesians 5:22–24

Are all women to submit to all men?

Session 4 – How to Be a Spouse 1

What could you do this week to serve your spouse. Is it possible to do this unconditionally (i.e. if he doesn't notice or say, "thank you," can you be content that you did this for the glory of God)? How could the group encourage you in this?

How might what you are learning about the scriptural commands for marriage be applicable to how our marriages reflect the relationship between Christ and the church?

During last session's Community Study and Discussion, you recorded how the group could help you on your journey towards spiritual maturity. Where have you struggled this week and where have you found success in your journey towards spiritual maturity? How could your community encourage you on the next steps?

... BE FILLED WITH THE SPIRIT ... GIVING THANKS ALWAYS AND FOR EVERYTHING TO GOD THE FATHER IN THE NAME OF OUR LORD JESUS CHRIST, SUBMITTING TO ONE ANOTHER OUT OF REVERENCE FOR CHRIST.

Ephesians 5:18, 20–21

Service

This week be thinking about how your group can help hurting marriages. Brainstorm as a group about how you might serve the marriages in your community. Ask your pastor(s) about current church programs that already exist to serve marriages. Are there any needs that your group can help meet over the next three weeks? Here are some ideas to get you started (perhaps nominate an individual to coordinate):

- Work with the church to offer a date night to the community. Volunteer to watch children, perhaps you can even help fund the date night and/or provide couples with talking points for dinner conversation.
- Host a small marriage retreat for couples in (or outside of) the church.
- Break into groups of 2–3 couples. Discuss how you could most positively influence each others' marriages. Perhaps the men could serve their wives by hosting a dinner (and the children could help). Perhaps the couples could commit to gathering together at each others' houses during the next month for dinner and conversation.

Other Ideas, Notes, Organization

Final page(s) for sketching, doodling, or additional thoughts / notes

Session 5 - Marriage: How to Be a Spouse II

Personal Study

Big Idea

IN BIBLICAL MARRIAGE, BOTH SPOUSES ARE CALLED TO PHYSICAL INTIMACY AND FAITHFULNESS. HUSBANDS SPECIFICALLY ARE CALLED TO LOVE THEIR WIVES; LEAVE CHILDHOOD; AND LIVE WITH THEIR WIVES IN GENTLENESS, UNDERSTANDING, AND HONOR. WIVES SPECIFICALLY ARE CALLED TO LOVE AND SUBMIT TO THEIR HUSBANDS, BE SELF-CONTROLLED, PURE, KIND, AND KEEP THE HOME.

Key Scripture

PSALM 66:18 | PROVERBS 5:15-22; 31:11 | 1 CORINTHIANS 7: 1-5
EPHESIANS 5:15-33 | COLOSSIANS 3:19 | TITUS 2:3-5 | 1 PETER 3:7

Read

CHAPTER 6 OF *THE RELATIONAL GOD*

Key Concepts (look for the answers to these questions while you read):

What are the two primary commands to which both husbands and wives should adhere?

_____

_____

_____

_____

_____

What else is commanded to husbands?

What else is commanded to wives?

What is the difference in the two words used for "love" in these passages (one for husbands and one for wives)?

What consequences might occur if men and women are not following these commands?

Just to review, what are the biblical commands governing marriage for

Both Spouses:

1. _____
2. _____

Husbands:

1. _____
2. _____
3. _____

Wives:

1. _____
2. _____

What do our marriages reflect when both spouses are following these commands? What do our marriages reflect when one or more spouses are not following these commands?

_____
_____
_____
_____
_____
_____
_____

Community Study and Discussion (men)

For this Community Study and Discussion, it might be best to split into groups of men and women if there are individuals who are willing to facilitate discussion.

At this point, we need to recognize that the body of Christ is diverse. Some of the individuals taking this study may be in a great marriage. Some marriages may be falling apart. Some may be divorced. Some may be single. That is okay. I would encourage you to not let your status keep you from the truths in God's word, because, remember, there is a purpose to studying the commands in Scripture for these relationships. Through these commands we can understand something about the nature and character of God. So, again, open-up and share with one another. Don't be afraid to learn from one another's experiences, both good and bad.

Last session you identified some things you were doing well and some areas where you could improve. Additionally, you identified some things you could do this past week to serve your wife (with the goal of doing them unconditionally). How did that go?

What are your thoughts about how you're doing as a husband after this past session's reading?

Let's review some of the concepts as we think about how to be more biblical husbands. Read Colossians 3:19 and 1 Peter 3:7. How do these verses add to the idea of *love* that we have been investigating?

What are the consequences of not following the commands in these passages?

Read Psalm 66:18. Why is this?

Have you ever seen these consequences play out in your life? How?

What are the opposite attitudes of the ones listed in these passages? When are you most likely to respond to your wife in that way?

How does the Bible say we should deal with those specific attitudes?

What could you do this week and in the long-term to implement biblical solutions to the attitudes in your life that lead to responding to your wife in a way opposite to that which we identified?

There are two other commands that are given to both spouses—physical intimacy and faithfulness. What unique challenges do you face as a husband when considering these two commands? Consider 1 Corinthians 7:1–5 and Proverbs 5:15–22 as you discuss.

What conversations do you need to have with your wife about this topic (while continuing to love, honor, and live with her in an understanding way)?

_____

_____

_____

_____

_____

_____

_____

Last session, you began thinking about what these commands to husbands and wives might mean when thinking about the relationship between Christ and the Church. Think more about that and record your thoughts and observations here.

_____

_____

_____

_____

_____

_____

_____

Community Study and Discussion (women)

For this Community Study and Discussion, it might be best to split into groups of men and women if there are individuals who are willing to facilitate discussion.

At this point, we need to recognize that the body of Christ is diverse. Some of the individuals taking this study may be in a great marriage. Some marriages may be falling apart. Some may be divorced. Some may be single. That is okay. I would encourage you to not let your status keep you from the truths in God's word, because, remember, there is a purpose to studying the commands in Scripture for these relationships. Through these commands we can understand something about the nature and character of God. So, again, open-up and share with one another. Don't be afraid to learn from one another's experiences, both good and bad.

Last session you identified some things you were doing well as well as areas you could improve. Additionally, you identified some things you could do this past week to serve your husband (with the goal of doing them unconditionally). How did that go?

What are your thoughts about how you're doing as a wife after this past session's reading?

Let's review some of the concepts as we think about how to be more biblical wives. Read Titus 2:3–5. How do these commands add to and compliment the concept of submission that we investigated last session?

What are the consequences of not following the commands in this passage?

Why is this?

Have you ever seen these consequences play out in your life? How?

Why do you think "older women" are commanded to teach/train these things?

What are the opposite attitudes of the ones listed in these passages? When are you most likely to respond to your husband in that way?

How does the Bible say we should deal with those specific attitudes?

What could you do this week and in the long-term to implement biblical solutions to the attitudes in your life that lead to responding to your husband in a way opposite to that which we identified?

There are two other commands that are given to both spouses—physical intimacy and faithfulness. What unique challenges do you face as a wife when considering these two commands? Consider 1 Corinthians 7:1–5 and Proverbs 31:11 as you discuss.

What conversations do you need to have with your husband about this topic (while continuing to love and submit to him)?

_____

_____

_____

Last session, you began thinking about what these commands to husbands and wives might mean when thinking about the relationship between Christ and the Church. Think more about that and record your thoughts and observations here.

_____

_____

_____

_____

_____

_____

_____

_____

_____

_____

Final page(s) for sketching, doodling, or additional thoughts / notes

Session 6 - Marriage: Christ and the Church

Personal Study

Big Idea

> OUR MARRIAGES ARE DESIGNED TO REFLECT CHRIST AND THE CHURCH, THE GODHEAD, AND SPIRITUAL COVENANT

Key Scripture

> LUKE 14:26 | JOHN 15 | ROMANS 7:1–6; 12:4–8 | 1 CORINTHIANS 7; 12
> EPHESIANS 5:22–32 | PHILIPPIANS 1:21 | COLOSSIANS 1:15–20
> REVELATION 19:6–9; 21:4, 9–11

Read

> CHAPTER 7 OF *THE RELATIONAL GOD*

Key Concepts (look for the answers to these questions while you read):

Our marriages were meant to reflect a deeper reality of Christ and the church. What is Christ's role in this now?

_____

_____

_____

_____

_____

_____

In the future?

What is our role in this now?

In the future?

From what unity does this love emanate?

What is the difference between Christ and Adam?

How does singleness bridge the gap between the physical reality and the spiritual reality?

> THIS MYSTERY IS PROFOUND, AND I AM SAYING THAT IT REFERS TO CHRIST AND THE CHURCH.
>
> Ephesians 5:32

Community Study and Discussion

What is the purpose of marriage? What purpose (conscious or unconscious) do you think your marriage is currently reflecting by the way you live? How does it need to change? How can your community help you?

How does knowing the reality of what our marriages are meant to reflect change your view of your own marriage?

Read Ephesians 5:22–32 again. Focus specifically on the role of Christ and the church. What actions do you see Christ taking towards the church? What action does the church take in these verses? Where do you need to *submit* to His authority in your life?

Notice, in verse 30, that Paul refers to us as the "body." There is certainly an individual aspect to this, but the bride of Christ refers to a corporate "body." Read Romans 12:4–8 and 1 Corinthians 12. These two passages identify how we are to live in the body. Read these lists. How has God gifted you? Pray about this. If you're not sure, ask a friend (or spouse). Also, pray about areas into which God may wish to stretch you:

_____

_____

_____

How are you using these gifts to edify the body? Is not doing so even an option? What excuses do you make to not exercise the gifts that the Lord has given you? Take some time this week to identify ways in which you might use your gifts. Perhaps speak with your pastor. If you don't have a pastor, it is time to get serious about being an active member of God's bride. Join a church. Use your gifts to strengthen the body

_____

_____

_____

Read 1 Corinthians 7. What does God's Word say about singleness? How does the church often treat singleness? How would your church or community treat Jesus or Paul if they were involved in your group? How do you need to change your viewpoint on singles in the church?

_____

_____

_____

During last session's "Community Study," you identified a few things that you could be working on to help grow your marriage. How are those coming?

_____

_____

Additionally, a few sessions ago, you identified some ways you could honor your parents in your current life season. What kind of progress have you made on those things?

_____

_____

The next session will examine the relationship of siblings. What do you think Scripture teaches about how we're to treat our brothers and sisters?

_____

_____

_____

There are *a lot* of siblings showcased in Scripture. What siblings can you think of in Scripture? What do they model for us?

_____

_____

_____

_____

Final page(s) for sketching, doodling, or additional thoughts / notes

Session 7 - Siblings: How to Be a Sibling

Personal Study

Big Idea

WE ARE BROTHERS AND SISTERS IN CHRIST AND WITH CHRIST; THEREFORE, WE ARE COMMANDED TO TREAT EACH OTHER IN CERTAIN WAYS.

Key Scripture

MATTHEW 7:3–5 | MARK 10:29–30
ROMANS 1:11–13; 8:14–17, 29; 13:8–9; 14–15:13; 15:25–30; 16:14
2 THESSALONIANS 3:15 | HEBREWS 2:5–3:6
1 JOHN 2:9–11; 3:10–12, 13–16; 4:20–21

Read

CHAPTERS 8 AND 9 OF *THE RELATIONAL GOD*

Key Concepts (look for the answers to these questions while you read):

What three points should we take from Hebrews 2:5–3:6?

What are the two different types of sibling relationships which Christ establishes through His work on the cross and resurrection from the dead?

The Relational God

How many times is the word *adelphos* **(brother) used in the New Testament? What are the three ways in which it is used?**

_____

_____

_____

When it is used to refer to a "spiritual brother" (i.e. a brother or sister *in Christ* **) what are the three categories?**

_____

_____

_____

What are the commands to our brothers and sisters *in Christ* **based on these three categories?**

_____

_____

_____

_____

_____

_____

_____

_____

Commands to brothers and sisters *in Christ* (cont.)?

Can we extrapolate those same commands to our physical brothers and sisters?

I APPEAL TO YOU, BROTHERS, BY THE NAME OF OUR LORD JESUS CHRIST, THAT ALL OF YOU AGREE, AND THAT THERE BE NO DIVISIONS AMONG YOU, BUT THAT YOU BE UNITED IN THE SAME MIND AND THE SAME JUDGMENT.

1 Corinthians 1:10

Community Study and Discussion

The reading examined Romans and Hebrews to identify the reason we can call one another brothers and sisters in Christ. What stood out to you about that study? How does that serve as the basis for our life together as brothers and sister in Christ?

During the last session you were challenged to identify your spiritual gifts. Please share those with the group. Write down the names of individuals with whom you share spiritual gifts and the names and gifts of individuals who have spiritual gifts in areas where you have weakness. How could these gifts be used to strengthen your local church? Take some time to share with one another specifically how you are using your spiritual gifts (or how you feel the Lord may be leading you to use your spiritual gifts) to build up His bride, the church.

How is the use of our gifts cross-applicable to what we are learning about brothers and sisters in Christ?

The reading identified six commands that are given to us as brothers and sisters in Christ. Which do you find easiest (mark with a ✓)? Which do you find most difficult (mark with an x)?

- ☐ **Warnings**
  [Matthew 18:15; Luke 17:3; Romans 15:14–15; 16:17; 1 Corinthians 5:11; Ephesians 4:15; 2 Thessalonians 3:15; 1 Timothy 5:1–2; James 5:19–20; 1 John 5:16]

- ☐ **Unifying Love through Peace, Reconciliation, and Eschewing Sinful Anger**
  [Matthew 5:22–24; 1 Corinthians 1:10–11, 6:1–8; Galatians 6:1; James 4:11; 1 Thessalonians 4:9–10; 1 John 2:9–11, 3:10–12, 13–16, 4:20–21]

- ☐ **Greeting, Visiting, and Keeping Their Company**
  [Mark 5:47; Luke 14:12; Acts 15:23, 36, 21:7, 28:14; Romans 1:11–13, 16:14; 1 Corinthians 16:20; Philippians 4:21; 1 Thessalonians 5:26; 2 Timothy 4:13, 21]

- ☐ **Supporting and Praying for One Another**
  [Acts 11:29; Romans 15:30; 1 Thessalonians 5:25; 2 Thessalonians 3:1 James 2:14–17; 1 John 3:17, 5:16; 3 John 5–8]

- ☐ **Being Equitable**
  [Matthew 7:3–5; Luke 6:41–42; Romans 13:1; Ephesians 6:5; 1 Thessalonians 5:12–13; 1 Timothy 6:1–2; Hebrews 13:17]

- ☐ **Misc. Commands (Forgiving, Strengthening, Comforting and Encouraging)**
  [Matthew 18:15–22; Luke 17:3–4, 22:32; Acts 15:32, 16:40; 1 Thessalonians 4:18, 5:11; 1 Timothy 5:1–2]

Read Romans 13:8–9. What should characterize our communities (our lives together)?

_____

_____

_____

_____

_____

_____

Now Read Romans 14–15:13 and answer the following questions:

How should we live with one another on non-essentials (vv. 14:18–19)?

Where have you been judgmental and need to repent (vv. 14:3–4, 10–13)?

Where have you flaunted your grace (made others stumble) and need to repent (14:3, 10–12)? Is it a matter for which you thank God, or simply an area where you want freedom (vv. 14:6, 23)? Can you live quietly in that freedom (vv. 14:22, 15:1–2)?

The Relational God

Do you have others who can challenge you without causing division/quarrelling (v. 14:1)? Have you given others in your community permission (and even invited) challenge?

_____
_____
_____
_____
_____

The next session will begin looking at what the Bible says to parents. What do you think the Bible commands parents to do?

_____
_____
_____

What cultural parenting practices do you think we often mistake for biblical practices?

_____
_____
_____

What is the fondest memory you have of parenting (or of being parented)?

_____
_____
_____
_____

Service

This is the last "Service" suggestion; however, since "Siblings" was only one session long, think about how you might specifically help parents (next session) with siblings. You may want to peak ahead at the commands given to parents. Then brainstorm about how you might serve the parents and siblings in your community. Ask your pastor(s) about current church programs that already serve parents and/or siblings. Are there any needs that your group can help meet over the next two weeks? Here are some ideas to get you started (perhaps nominate an individual to coordinate):

- Work with the church to offer a family friendly night for the community.
- Work with your church to identify a ministry that serves children who do not have parents. Ask that ministry how you might help.
- If you're willing to be involved for the long-term consider the following:
    - Research and discover how your church, your group, or you individually can be involved in helping eliminate the number of children in foster care in your community.
    - Consider partnering with your church to identify children within the church who are missing one or more of their parents and start a mentoring program where church members can pour into the lives of those children.
    - Most states have a mandate that child welfare agencies make efforts to allow siblings who are in their care to see one another monthly (if they are in separate foster families or facilities). Unfortunately, there is often not enough resources to make this happen. Meet with state welfare officials to see how you might help facilitate siblings getting to see one another (or identify other needs that the agency might have).
- Break into groups of 2–3 couples. Discuss how you could positively influence each others' parenting. Perhaps fathers could create tangible *memorials* or *rituals* for their children together. Perhaps mothers could discuss tangible ways to show love to their children in a group setting.

Other Ideas, Notes, Organization

Final page(s) for sketching, doodling, or additional thoughts / notes

Session 8 - Parents: How to Be a Parent

Personal Study

Big Idea

PARENTS ARE COMMANDED TO TEACH AND DISCIPLINE THEIR CHILDREN. FATHERS SPECIFICALLY ARE COMMANDED TO BE GENTLE WITH THEIR CHILDREN. MOTHERS SPECIFICALLY ARE COMMANDED TO LOVE THEIR CHILDREN.

Key Scripture

DEUTERONOMY 6:1–9 | PROVERBS 13:24; 19:18 | EPHESIANS 6:4 | TITUS 2:4

Read

CHAPTERS 10 AND 11 OF *THE RELATIONAL GOD*

Key Concepts (look for the answers to these questions while you read):

What three things are you (as a father or as a mother) commanded to do in Scripture?

What is the best way to learn something?

How should we be teaching our children? What is the purpose of teaching our children (particularly considering what we discovered was the goal of childhood in session 1)?

What is the purpose of discipline? How should discipline be used?

Fathers, what does it mean to not be harsh with your children?

Why is this particular command given to fathers?

Mothers, what sort of love should you provide to your children? How is that different than the love we have discussed up to this point in the study?

How does this love (*philos* – brotherly love) compare to the commands we saw to siblings in last session's study?

Why is this particular command given to mothers?

The Relational God

AND THESE WORDS THAT I COMMAND YOU TODAY SHALL BE ON YOUR HEART. YOU SHALL TEACH THEM DILIGENTLY TO YOUR CHILDREN, AND SHALL TALK OF THEM WHEN YOU SIT IN YOUR HOUSE, AND WHEN YOU WALK BY THE WAY, AND WHEN YOU LIE DOWN, AND WHEN YOU RISE.

Deuteronomy 6:6–7

Community Study and Discussion

If you could change one thing about your parenting, what would it be? What is going well that you could strengthen, what is going poorly that you could correct? Is what you're concerned about actually biblical?

The reading considered making *memorials* for your children. What kind of memorials do you remember from your own childhood. What sort of memorials does your family have now? What sort of memorials could you set up for your children?

The reading considered discipline being an extension of teaching (teaching with consequences). What has been your previous experience with discipline (both as a child and as a parent)? How should that change?

Fathers, take a few minutes to examine your own heart. When are you most likely to be harsh? What steps can you take to guard against harshness?

Fathers, read Ephesians 6:4, Colossians 3:21, Proverbs 15:1, and Hebrews 2:11. Now think about your own household. Which characteristics from these verses are most often present?

Mothers, take a few minutes to examine your own heart. How are you doing showing your children a *philos* sort of love? When are you most likely to give or not give that sort of love to your child?

There will be those in the group with different age children. How do these or have these commands affected your parenting as your children have grown? What did you do well? What do you wish you had done differently? What wisdom can you provide the group?

Infant

Preschool

Grade School

Teenager

Adults

Final page(s) for sketching, doodling, or additional thoughts / notes

Session 9 - Parents: The Mother and Father Heart of God

Personal Study

Big Idea

AS WE GROW IN THE LORD, WE HAVE THE RESPONSIBILITY TO BE SPIRITUAL PARENTS. OUR ROLES AS BOTH PHYSICAL AND SPIRITUAL PARENTS REFLECT THE MOTHER AND FATHER HEART OF GOD.

Key Scripture

MATTHEW 6:9–13; 7:7–11; 28:19 | JOHN 15:12–16 | ROMANS 8:15
COLOSSIANS 1:15 | TITUS 3:3–7 | HEBREWS 12:5–11 | JAMES 3:17–18 |
REVELATION 3:19

Read

CHAPTER 12 OF *THE RELATIONAL GOD*

Key Concepts (look for the answers to these questions while you read):

What responsibility do we have to advance the kingdom of God through making disciples?

How does God fulfill all the commands given to parents?

What are specific *fatherly* attributes which God demonstrates? How does that help you more fully understand His nature and character?

What are specific *motherly* attributes which God demonstrates? How does that help you more fully understand His nature and character?

How do we see Christ demonstrate the *philos* aspects of love that are attributed to mothers in the Titus passage we covered last session?

> AND BECAUSE YOU ARE SONS, GOD HAS SENT THE SPIRIT OF HIS SON INTO OUR HEARTS, CRYING, "ABBA! FATHER!"
>
> Galatians 4:6

Community Study and Discussion

What struggles have you had envisioning God as a parent?

The reading mentioned "spiritual parenting." This, necessarily, starts at home with our own children. Intentionality is important in parenting. What do you want for your child spiritually in their current season? In future seasons? Have you prayed about whether this is what God wants for you child? How can you help facilitate that?

Perhaps you do not have children (or even if you do), are there children in the church who could benefit from having additional spiritual guidance in their lives? How could you help facilitate that?

How are the commands given to parents (teaching, discipline, love, and/or gentleness) cross-applicable to spiritual parenting?

How does God demonstrate those commands in His interactions with us? Use Scripture to support your answers.

Are you willing to share a time where you felt the discipline of the Lord in your life? How have you personally experienced the other attributes of "parent" that we discussed last session (teaching, love, and/or gentleness) in your relationship with God?

The reading considered how our physical relationships reflect spiritual realities about the nature and character of God to explain difficult to understand concepts (like prayer and generosity). What other theological concepts might be helped by considering them in the light of our own created relationships?

Why are we able to be seen as sons and daughters of God? The answer to this is the culmination of all the concepts in this study!

Final page(s) for sketching, doodling, or additional thoughts / notes

Session 10 - Adoption: A New Forever Family

Personal Study

Big Idea

IT IS ONLY THROUGH ADOPTION THAT WE ARE ABLE TO BE PART OF GOD'S FAMILY. ADOPTION IS THE FINISHING TOUCH ON THE MASTERPIECE OF A METAPHOR THAT GOD HAS BREATHED INTO HIS CREATION. LOOK TO YOUR RELATIONSHIPS. WHERE YOU HAVE PROBLEMS INTERPERSONALLY, YOU MAY DISCOVER THOSE SAME TENDENCIES TO BE THORNY AREAS SPIRITUALLY.

Key Scripture

ROMANS 8:14–17 | GALATIANS 4:4–7 | EPHESIANS 1:3–10; 5–6:4

Read

CONCLUSION AND AFTERWORD OF *THE RELATIONAL GOD*

Key Concepts (look for the answers to these questions while you read):

How is physical adoption different from spiritual adoption?

How do the Old Testament and New Testament concepts of adoption differ?

What is the role of Christ in our adoption as sons and daughters of God?

How does the idea of adoption in Christ synthesize these two concepts?

Community Study and Discussion

How have you personally been affected by adoption? Was it a good experience or a bad experience? In what ways does your experience reflect the spiritual concept of adoption found in the Bible? In what ways is it different?

Compare Romans 8:14–17 with Galatians 4:4–7 and Ephesians 1:3–10. What do you notice about spiritual adoption?

Now we will spend some time reviewing and reflecting on the content of the entire study, and you will have one last chance to apply these concepts to your life.

What are the three primary commands for children?

Where could you personally improve in your relationship as a child (spiritually or physically)?

What are the seven primary commands for marriage?

Where could you personally improve in your relationship as a spouse (spiritually or physically)?

What are the eight inferences in Scripture about how we should treat our brothers and sisters (in Christ)?

Where could you personally improve in your relationship as a sibling (spiritually or physically)?

What are the four primary commands for parents?

Where could you personally improve in your relationship as a parent (spiritually or physically)?

How does your status as an adopted son or daughter of God change your outlook on your position in the family of God?

Final page(s) for sketching, doodling, or additional thoughts / notes

A Concluding Letter from the Author

At the outset of this study, I encouraged you to examine why you were here and what you hoped to gain from this study. I would encourage you to go review your answers to those questions. Have you accomplished what you had hoped?

Whether you have accomplished everything you set out to accomplish or not, I challenged you in that opening letter (and in the final lesson) that:

> **WHERE YOU HAVE PROBLEMS INTERPERSONALLY, YOU MAY DISCOVER THOSE SAME TENDENCIES AS THORNY AREAS SPIRITUALLY.**

Have you been able to identify some of those areas? What steps are you taking to grow in your walk with the Lord (both individually and with the accountability of your brothers and sisters in Christ)?

It is my hope and prayer that this study has deepened your relationships with your family and your walk with Christ.

I would love to hear your stories and your thoughts and comments about this Bible study. My contact information is below.

Grace and Peace,

--Steven J. Halbert

- 📧 shalbert@tusitalapublishers.com

- 🌐 https://www.stevenhalbert.com

- 𝗮 https://www.amazon.com/author/stevenhalbert

Appendix A - Book: Intro through Chapter 2

Introduction

My wife and I have often joked that our kids came with fewer instructions than did the car seats in which we brought them home. But, when I think about it, that statement is true for all of our relationships, isn't it?

There's no instruction manual.

This book was born out of a desire to understand what God's Word says about how the relationships that He created (children, spouses, siblings, and parents) thrive.

As the book progressed, two surprising themes emerged. First, there were far fewer commands governing these relationships than I anticipated. And, second, Scripture uses these relationships as metaphors, and the commands that govern these relationships reveal truths about the nature and character of God.

As you can imagine then, this book has been a long time coming. I have started and stopped it more than four times over the last ten years because of the very topic this book is about—relationships.

And relationships take time.

I am a son, a brother, a husband, and a father. Each of these relationships is dynamic and has required more or less of my energy during the past ten years, so I stop writing and the book sits idle for another year. Yet, there is something about the concepts in this book that I just can't shake. I feel called to write them. Part of the reason I feel this calling is because there is no condensed resource that handles all of these relationships at once. But that is also part of the problem. So much can be said about each one of these relationships that the enormity of the task muddles my thinking until, little by little, the book devolves into something akin to stream of consciousness.

But now the book is here. It's done!

And it's done due in no small part to my Sunday school class and my wife. My Sunday school class graciously agreed to allow me to use the concepts from this book as our topic over a several-month period, which helped provide much needed structure for those topics while focusing my writing on what others found applicable.[1] Additionally, my wife agreed to let me spend some time writing over the course of the last few months, and the combination of those two things seem to have provided enough time and focus to birth a book. So what is this book actually about?

The Relational God

The genesis of this book was relatively simple. It began with a question:

If God could have created us to be in any sort of relationships that He wanted, why did He create us to be children, spouses, parents, and siblings?

Think about that for a minute.

God created this world, in particular humans, to function within a specific relational framework. He could have created us in any way that He wanted. We could have been amoeba-like, able to simply split ourselves in half to form new selves. We could have come out of the womb fully functioning, without any need for parents. We could have been allowed to reproduce only once. And a myriad of other

Introduction

possibilities, which would drastically change the way we relate to one another. Yet God created us to function within the specific relational frameworks of children, spouses, siblings, and parents.

So why did God create us like this?

That is the question this book seeks to answer. It seeks to answer it by examining each of the relationships mentioned above: child, spouse, sibling, and parent. They are explored in that order intentionally because, with the exception of siblings, we generally progress through those relationships in that order. First, we are children. Next, we may become a spouse (but we may not). After that, we may become parents (or again, we may not). Finally, since the relationship of sibling is relatively fluid, I place it between spouse and parent because our experience as a sibling changes throughout the first three relational realities; nevertheless, our identity as a sibling remains something of a constant, and the spiritual metaphors are more powerful when considered within such a framework.

These relationships compose a large majority of our relational capacity; but, too often, we take them for granted. We treat them as an afterthought—until there is a problem. Then we become interested in focusing our time, energy, and resources on making them work. Yet most of Scripture commands a steady faithfulness, so that these relationships function well and even thrive.

Structure

The Relational God is divided into four sections, which explore each of the four relationships (child, spouse, sibling, and parent) in three ways: experience, commands, and metaphors.

In the first chapter of each section, we explore our *experiences* in each of these roles, and we also examine three or four biblical narratives that embody those relationships. I have chosen specific biblical narratives to which I can return in multiple sections, and, while there are countless other biblical examples to cite, I tried to choose narratives that could provide a well-rounded picture throughout the book.

The second chapter in each section explores what the Bible *commands* practically for these roles (to help redeem and sanctify some of our *experiences*). In section 2, "Spouses," this actually takes two chapters, and in section 3, "Siblings," it is combined with what is typically the final chapter.

The final chapter of each section explores what those relationships—when practiced biblically—tell us about God. Ultimately, this book is driven by the premise that God created us within a specific relational framework. When those relationships are healthy and thriving, they reveal important aspects about the nature and character of God. The relationships themselves become living *metaphors*.

Personal History

Before we begin, however, I want to give you a little background about me. All of us have a relational history that biases our view of various relationships, so I think it is important for you to know my background before we dive into this book.

My name is Steven Halbert. I was born in the early eighties to Tim and Donna Halbert in Fresno, California. My dad, Tim, grew up as a preacher's kid with two siblings—a brother and a sister—and he lived in nearly every area of the country. My mom, Donna, grew up in a hardworking middle-class Michigan family with four siblings—all girls.

My dad had a career in sales, and my mom circulated between various professional jobs and being a stay-at-home-mom. My home life was a very stable Christian environment. My parents did a great job.

When I was seven years old, our family adopted an infant girl. Shortly thereafter, we moved from California to South Carolina, where I grew up and attended elementary, middle, and high school. I spent two years at a Bible college (also in South Carolina) before transferring to a state school.

After college, I started work as a houseparent at a group home. I lived with and helped raise six to eight middle school boys who were in the foster care system. That was a tall order for someone just coming out of college, and it grew me up fast.

About six months after starting work, I met my future wife, Michelle, at a conference. Michelle and I dated for two months before I was accepted into grad school and invited her to come with me. In less than one year, I met and married Michelle, and we moved to Alabama, where I attended grad school for two years and received an MA in English while Michelle worked as a girl's youth director at a local church. Once my graduate program ended, we moved back to South Carolina where I began work as the director of children's services at a local nonprofit that had seventy-five to a hundred children in foster care on any given night.

After two years and several months of being back in South Carolina, Michelle gave birth to our daughter, Sophie. I will never forget that she told me she was pregnant on April Fools' Day.

In August of the next year, I left that ministry and started a job in marketing at a local manufacturer. Two years later, Michelle gave birth to our son, Andrew. I remember his birthday because it is *exactly* halfway to Christmas—prime position to receive the maximum amount of presents from doting grandparents. I still work for that manufacturer, but my role has changed to that of a product manager.

That is my life in a nutshell. Many stories in this book are derived from my life and experiences, and now you have a framework in which to place those stories. This is important because the defining moments in all of our lives center around people. Even when we think that a moment centers on our careers or a particular accomplishment, it is typically the relationships shaping those career experiences or life

accomplishments that stand the test of time and outlast the moment itself. That is why focusing on our relationships is so critical.

Having an understanding of the frame in which a story appears is also important with the stories we will examine from Scripture. Thus, it is paramount to have an understanding of the metanarrative of Scripture.

The metanarrative is the overarching story of Scripture: creation, fall, and redemption. All the individual stories in the Bible fall within this overarching structure. Indeed, since we have not yet seen the culmination of all the things described in Revelation, your story and mine fall within the metanarrative of Scripture as well. Ours is the story of God reaching out and desiring a relationship with us. We are in the middle of what theologians often refer to as the "already, but not yet." In other words, the kingdom of God is among us. We are adopted into God's family through the work of Christ, but the culmination of that kingdom and that family is not fully realized until Christ's return.

> The defining moments in all of our lives center around people.

That is why understanding the relational metaphors in Scripture is so important and powerful in our lives. It helps us better understand and anticipate what is coming. God has left us nuggets of truths in our relationships that point to His kingdom, just as He did when He walked this earth. All you have to do is open the Bible app on your phone and search, "the kingdom of heaven is like." You will get quite a few results directly from Jesus' mouth.

They are all metaphors.

And Jesus created everything that He uses as a metaphor. So let's see what these four relationships—relationships created by God—can help us understand about God and our relationship with Him.

Part One
Children:
Sons and Daughters

Being a Child:
Our Shared Experience

We are all children. This is the one relationship to which all of humanity can relate. You are someone's child. I am someone's child. So let's talk about our experience as children.

Experience

What pops into your head when you think about your own childhood? If you're like me, you have a lot of snapshots. Brief snippets of life that have stuck with you.

For me, those snapshots include playing tag on the playground at my elementary school. I was fast—really fast. And I would taunt the other kids.

They include memories of getting into trouble starting in the fifth grade, which led my parents to enroll me in a Christian middle school where I stayed until I graduated from high school.

I think about the neighborhood where I grew up. During the winters, I came home from school, dropped off my backpack, grabbed my dog, and headed into the woods until dinner. During summers, I left the house at 8:00 a.m. for swim practice at the neighborhood pool, walked home to eat lunch, and then returned to the pool until dinner. I *loved* to swim.

I think about mowing lawns, washing cars, and watering plants for neighbors to earn money.

I think about my friends.

I think about being mentored by a former professional billiards player. The lessons he taught me and my friends have remained with me to this day.

I had a great childhood. My parents were good people. My father provided for our family, and my mother took good care of us. It was ideal.

Maybe you were like me. Maybe you had Christian parents—not perfect people, but good people who took good care of you. Maybe your parents were not Christians, but you still had a great childhood. Or maybe your childhood was painful, the complete opposite of my experience.

In the introduction, I mentioned my work in foster care. I have worked with lots of children who have had the complete opposite experience of my childhood. I think about Tobias and Pablo, a pair of brothers who came into care at one of the facilities where I worked. Their mother was in another country, and their father was in a US prison.

Tobias and Pablo were adopted when they were five and seven years old. Prior to that, they had been in three homes in three years. When they were eight and ten, their adoptive family broke apart and "gave them back." No joke.

They also had a thirteen-year-old brother, Jorge, who was in and out of juvenile detention. The first few times that Jorge entered juvie was due to violence from protecting his kid brothers. Tobias and Pablo loved Jorge. They idolized him and desperately wanted to see him.

When they first came to my house, Tobias and Pablo were quite disruptive. The youngest, Tobias, suffered from depression because of

Being a Child

internalized guilt over the adoptive family falling apart and "returning them." Pablo, on the other hand, often acted out aggressively, attempting to get under the skin of the staff or manipulate the other kids in the house.

Over time, and with lots of focused work, these two began to stabilize and achieve some level of normalcy within the house. But after a few months of stability, it's as if something snapped within Pablo. He began testing the limits and pushing the envelope to see if we, too, would give up on him.

His actions grew more and more aggressive and inappropriate, and they culminated in some behaviors that the home for which I was working was unequipped to handle. I poured blood, sweat, and tears into those two. I did everything in my power to keep them together. And I fought for Pablo to stay—despite several offers from management to move him to another facility. I knew what it would do to Tobias if they were separated.

The day they decided to take Pablo to another placement, I wrote one word in my journal. I am a very articulate individual without much use for profanity. The word I wrote in my journal that day was what spiraled into a deep depression that took several months to overcome.

I wish that story had a happy ending. I don't know what happened to those two. I look for them on social media from time to time, but ultimately, their story is lost to me.

Maybe your childhood was full of pain and disappointment like theirs. The truth is that our collective experiences as children are vast.

But we are all children.

Most of our childhood stories will fall somewhere between mine and Tobias and Pablos. So what's the point?

What is the point of childhood?
What is the "job" of all children?

The Relational God

It is—essentially—to grow up.

My own children, Sophie and Andrew, are going through a Peter Pan phase right now. Remember the story? John and Michael are playing imaginatively in the "nursery" while their sister, Wendy, is caught between the worlds of children and grown-ups. From the very first lines of the story, we learn that growing up is inevitable, and Wendy is caught amid that struggle. Enter Peter Pan in the middle of the night to whisk the children to Neverland, where they will never grow up.

Can you imagine never "growing up"? That is what makes J. M. Barrie's story resonate with so many. It leaves us with a rather interesting question, doesn't it?

What does it mean to "grow up"?[1]

When I presented this question to my Sunday school class, one notable response was that we strive for independence despite reality. In other words, childhood becomes one long journey (or struggle) toward independence. Often that journey moves more slowly than we would like, but, in other situations, the opposite might be true.

Depending on who you ask, "growing up" or "becoming a man" or "becoming a woman" comes at different milestones. Ultimately, as we will see in the next chapter, growing up is represented by a certain level of independence and autonomy from our parents. Yet one of the hallmarks of being a "child" in Scripture is faith. Our vocabulary even has the phrase "childlike faith" precisely because of what Scripture has to say about being a child. Indeed, *faith* is the hallmark of childhood, and *trust* is the foundation of faith.

Children implicitly trust the adults in their lives to do those things that are good and right, and they are often oblivious to any opposite reality.[2] Childlike faith, then, is applying this unencumbered trust to our relationship with God. But can we maintain childlike faith while maturing spiritually? Let's look at three different biblical stories that might help answer this question, as well as shape our idea of what being a child means.

Biblical Examples

These are stories to which we will return throughout the book, so pay careful attention in this initial description because I refer back to these narratives in other sections as well. In this chapter, I will spend the most time on Joseph since his story and the stories of his family will be considered in every section of the book.

Joseph

Joseph's story spans thirteen chapters of Scripture from Genesis 37–50. Early in the story, we learn that Joseph is the youngest of Jacob's eleven sons. Jacob played favorites, and he made Joseph a special robe to denote his favoritism. Then he sent him to check on his brothers, to make sure they were doing their job as shepherds. Joseph brought back negative reports. Genesis 37:4 says that his brothers "hated him and could not speak peacefully to him."

To make matters worse, Joseph had two dreams, which he shared with his brothers and parents. Both dreams implied that his entire family would bow down to him. As you can imagine, this did not help his relationship with his brothers.

After this episode with the dreams, Jacob again sends Joseph to check on his brothers. As he approaches the field where they are keeping their sheep, his brothers devise a plot to kill him; however, one of the brothers, Reuben, tells them not to kill him, but, rather, to throw him into a pit in the wilderness. Genesis 37:22 tells us that Reuben intended to rescue him.

But he did not have the chance.

The rest of Joseph's brothers (led by Judah—the eldest) conspire to sell Joseph to a group of traders. So when Reuben returns to the pit to rescue Joseph, he is already gone. All the brothers then fall party to the same plan. They decide to kill a goat; dip Joseph's special robe in the blood; present it to their father, Jacob; and lead him to believe they found it in the wilderness. Upon seeing the bloodied coat, Jacob mourns for "many days"—even saying that he will die of grief (Genesis 37:34–35).

Meanwhile, Joseph is forced into his growing-up moment. He is no longer under the protection and care of his father's household. He is taken to Egypt, and the captain of Pharaoh's guards, Potiphar, purchases him as a servant. The next part of the story shows how God takes care of Joseph in many of the situations in which he finds himself.

Joseph rises in prominence as a servant and overseer of Potiphar's house, until he is running the whole house. Potiphar's wife attempts to seduce him, and he flees. She lies about the seduction, claiming that Joseph intended to rape her, so Joseph is thrown into jail.

God is with Joseph, who is placed in a position of leadership within the prison. He attends to some high-level government officials who have fallen out of favor with Pharaoh. With the Lord's help, Joseph interprets the chief cupbearer and the chief baker's dreams, and the interpretations become reality. The chief cupbearer is restored, and the chief baker is executed—just as Joseph said.

Joseph requests that the chief cupbearer appeal to Pharaoh on his behalf, but the chief cupbearer never mentions Joseph to Pharaoh until Pharaoh is bothered by a dream. *Then* the chief cupbearer remembers Joseph and informs Pharaoh that someone can interpret his dreams. Joseph is able to interpret Pharaoh's dream about an upcoming famine; therefore, Pharaoh places Joseph as second-in-command in all of Egypt, in charge of preparing for the upcoming famine.

At this point in the story, Joseph is thirty years old. When the story began, Joseph was seventeen years old. He has been away from his family for thirteen years, and he effectively prepares an entire nation for a famine. As Pharaoh's dreams predicted, there are seven years of prosperity followed by seven years of famine (so Joseph is thirty-seven when the famine begins). During the years of prosperity, Joseph has two sons—Manasseh and Ephraim.

Under Joseph's leadership, Egypt is so prepared for the famine that once the famine hits, his family (many miles away) gets word that Egypt has grain. Thus, Joseph's brothers travel down to Egypt to buy some grain. At this point, it has been over twenty years since the episode between Joseph and his brothers. They all have families, and Joseph has assimilated into a new culture.

When the brothers come before Joseph, they do not recognize him, but he recognizes them. They bow before him, and Scripture says that Joseph "remembered the dreams that he had dreamed of them" (Genesis 42:9). He accuses them of being spies and throws them in jail for three days. After the three days, he demands that they go home and return with their youngest brother, Benjamin, because, during their initial questioning, they informed Joseph that they had a younger half-brother (Joseph's full brother, whom he has never met). Just to be sure, he keeps one of the brothers—Simeon—in custody, as collateral.

Upon returning home, the brothers want to take their youngest brother, Benjamin, back to Egypt immediately to recover Simeon, but Jacob will not allow it. Hunger is a powerful motivator, though; and, once the food runs out, Jacob relents. As they prepare to leave, one of Jacob's sons, Judah, swears that no harm shall befall Benjamin, and the brothers head back to Egypt to buy food and recover Simeon.

Upon their arrival, Joseph orders a feast. Just prior to the feast, when Joseph meets Benjamin for the first time, he is so overcome with emotion that he excuses himself to weep. At the feast, he seats them according to their ages. He feasts with them, and then fills their sacks with grain and sends them on their way—this time *with* Simeon. However, Joseph has his royal cup placed in Benjamin's sack, so he can have an excuse to take his younger brother captive. He sends men after them to seize (or rescue) Benjamin. But Judah offers himself in Benjamin's place—the very Judah who masterminded the plot to sell Joseph into slavery in the first place.

Again, Joseph is overcome with emotion, but instead of excusing himself, this time he orders all of his attendants out of the room. And he "made himself known to his brothers. And he wept aloud" (Genesis 45:1–2). After this emotional reunion, the brothers return home.

Can you imagine the sort of "coming clean" meeting these brothers would have had with their father, Jacob? They sold their brother into slavery, and lived with the lie that he was dead for more than twenty years. Once they convince Jacob that Joseph is alive and, in fact, ruler of Egypt, they all move their families to settle in the land of Goshen, which Joseph secures from Egypt to protect them from the famine.

This is a tragic story with a beautiful ending. When he was in Jacob's home, Joseph was loved more than his brothers, and he even had the audacity to share his dream of the family bowing to him—despite the fact that he was the youngest son and had not accomplished anything deserving of such an honor. Yet, by the end of the story, he honors his father by becoming the provider. He brings the entire family to Egypt and humbly provides for their needs. He could have allowed bitterness to rule his heart. He could have had every one of his brothers executed. Instead, he honors and provides for his family. The turning point for Joseph—moving from a favorite son and an entitled ruler to an honoring son and a humble provider—seems to be the birth of his own sons.

Genesis 41:51 tells us that "Joseph called the name of the firstborn Manasseh. 'For,' he said, 'God has made me forget all my hardship and all my father's house.'" The footnote in my Bible indicates that "*Manasseh* sounds like the Hebrew for *making to forget*."

This family was incredibly dysfunctional, yet their story makes it into the canon of Scripture for us to see and study. No matter your experience, God uses the relationships in your life to advance His purposes and speak truths about Himself and His character into your life. Imagine if Joseph were telling you his story. You would likely be listening with incredulity as he explained how his brothers tried to kill him, sold him into slavery, and then groveled before him as a ruler. None of us would have faulted Joseph if he had chosen to take vengeance.

> Joseph goes from a favorite son and an entitled ruler to an honoring son and a humble provider.

But he doesn't.

He lets God redeem his experience.

Your experience as a child may not have been perfect, but God can still redeem that experience. The story of Joseph is one of God redeeming dysfunction. Now we will swing the pendulum in the opposite direction and examine the childhood of Jesus.

Jesus

Standard systematic theology teaches that Jesus is 100 percent man and 100 percent God;[3] thus, He provides a perfect example of how to be a child. Because we are concerned about growing up and developing a sense of autonomy, I want to focus on two distinct moments in Scripture as they concern Jesus. The first is found in Luke 2:41–52.

Jesus' family goes to Jerusalem annually for the Feast of the Passover. When Jesus is twelve years old, His family leaves the feast without Him. A group is traveling together, and his mom and dad just assume He is among the other travelers. He is not.[4]

It takes Mary and Joseph an entire day to realize that Jesus is not with them. When they do, they return to Jerusalem to look for Him. Scripture tells us that Jesus is on His own for at least three days, and His parents finally discover Him in the temple, "sitting among the teachers, listening to them and asking them questions" (Luke 2:46). When they reprimand Him, Jesus responds, "Why were you looking for me? Did you not know that I must be in my Father's house?" (v. 49).

This astonishing reply points to a truth that we frequently miss as children. We fight so hard for independence; yet Jesus models a new dependence on a new Father. He drives this point home years later when He is teaching on prayer. When His disciples ask Him to teach them to pray, He says, "When you pray, say: 'Father . . .'" (Luke 11:2). He tells His disciples to approach God as a "father." Someone who can handle your requests.

Similarly, in the previous story, Joseph is quick to acknowledge to the officials of Egypt that the Lord is the source of dream interpretation. Joseph goes from telling dreams to his family that *imply* one set of outcomes to relying on the Lord for the *interpretation* and *fulfillment* of those outcomes.

"Growing up," then, is not about gaining independence at all. Rather, it is about switching dependence from one set of caretakers to the ultimate Caretaker.

And Jesus models that process. Indeed, Luke tells us that after Mary and Joseph located Jesus, He "went down with them and came to Nazareth and was submissive to them" (Luke 2:51). We will cover this idea later, but, for now, just understand that this represents a shift from *obedience* to *submission*. Thus, the process of Jesus' shifting dependence from his earthly parents to his heavenly Father seems to begin here and culminate at His baptism, where the heavens open and a voice claims, "You are my beloved Son; with you I am well pleased" (Luke 3:22).

In a similar incident six chapters later, Jesus is transfigured right before the very eyes of three of His disciples, and a voice comes out of a cloud saying, "This is my Son, my Chosen One; listen to him" (Luke

9:35). In this passage, God the Father claims Jesus directly, with all the authority of Himself. He commands that we "listen to Him." No other biblical figure is given that kind of latitude with his or her life. God sanctions all things done by Jesus.

In Jesus, then, we have the perfect model for the journey of childhood. Rather than a long, arduous journey to independence, Jesus models that we are to shift our dependence from our earthly parents to our heavenly Father. But before we move on to what the Bible actually commands for children, let's take a look at two more children in a single story.

The Prodigal Son

This story contains quite possibly one of the most well-known children in the Bible: the Prodigal Son. He has an older brother, though. And the contrast is stunning when examined in light of the idea of shifting dependence because it changes our understanding of which son is actually the prodigal.

The story of the prodigal son can be found in Luke 15:11–32. It begins with a younger son telling his father that he wants his inheritance early. He attempts to force his independence at the expense of his father and older sibling. His father complies and gives him the inheritance, which he squanders on "reckless living" in a "far country" (Luke 15:13). He then ends up hiring himself out to citizens of that country to feed the pigs. His wages are minimal to nonexistent considering he finds himself longing for the pigs' food.

Countless commentaries, sermons, and blog posts explain just how shocking this would have been to Jesus' Jewish audience. From demanding an inheritance early (as the youngest son, no less!) to a nice Jewish boy sitting among the pigs, I will not rehash all of those societal taboos here. The point I want to emphasize is that it is not until he comes to his senses and places his dependence on the mercy of the father that he gains true freedom.

Since this is a parable, the metaphor is a bit tricky because the physical father in the story is also a representation of our spiritual Father. In the parable, the father finds a broken, contrite, and truly dependent child. A child who finally acknowledges, "I have sinned against heaven and before you. I am no longer worthy to be called your son" (Luke 15:21). He has finally learned true dependence. His future generational wealth is gone. He cannot hope in it. He can hope only in the father's love, and he must live daily in that hope.

And what does the father do? He does what (hopefully) any father would do. He embraces him and celebrates the heart change. The lesson here is crystal clear: we are to approach our heavenly Father this way. Unfortunately, our hearts are more often like the older brother's.

We are aware of the older brother from the very first sentence of the story: "There was a man who had two sons'" (Luke 15:11), but we don't actually meet him until the end of the story. During this time, the older brother is dutifully in the field (v. 25). He does not even receive an invite to the party that the father throws in celebration of the younger brother's return! When the older brother learns of the party, "he [is] angry and refuse[s] to go in" (v. 28). The father pleads with the older brother to come celebrate, and he reminds the older brother that everything else that the father owns belongs to him. But the older brother has already deducted the calf and the robe from the mental balance sheet of his inheritance. He is resentful and accuses the father of being ungrateful and ungenerous. His heart is the same as the younger brother's was at the start of the story! It just manifests itself differently.

The story ends with the father reminding the older brother that "it was fitting to celebrate and be glad, for this your brother was dead, and is alive; he was lost, and is found" (v. 32). Yet it is the older brother who is now lost. His heart is far from the father.

Conclusion

Our common story as children turns out to be not so common after all. God created the parent-child relationship to teach us something about Himself and His relationship to us. These examples demonstrate that what God wants from His children are their hearts.

Dependence on Him.

Spiritual maturity, then, is contingent upon increasing our childlike faith. Depending so fully on God that all other influences are secondary. Let's think, therefore, about *why* and *how* we can increase our dependence upon God by examining what He commands tactically in His Word for all of us as children.

How to Be a Child: What Scripture Says

Because we are all children, we all approach God's Word with our own histories. That is why the stories included in His Word are so precious. They take away our excuses. The Bible is replete with stories about children in far worse situations than our own.

And still it contains the commands.

It is as if the stories in God's Word are built-in empathy. The commands may be difficult—and God understands that your story may be particularly difficult (just think about the biblical example of Joseph in the last chapter)—but the commands are there nonetheless. What we cannot forget, though, is that God's desire for His children is not independence, but, rather, a shift in dependence. He wants our hearts.

These commands help with that.

So what does the Bible have to say about being a child?

What are the commands to children?

What you will find as we go through these chapters is that the Bible has surprisingly few commands when it comes to the tactical outworking of these relationships. And, while the amount may be small, actually doing them is no small task.

As far as I can tell, there are only three commands for children in the Bible:

1. Honor
2. Obey
3. Learn

So let's take a look at each of these directives. We'll start with the Ten Commandments.

Honor

The fifth commandment in Exodus 20:12 reads,

> Honor your father and your mother, that your days may be long in the land that the LORD your God is giving you.

In Exodus 20, God lays a foundation that will help His people thrive (long life in a chosen land). This command to honor your father and mother is in the middle of a list of commandments that we generally think of as targeting adults (don't murder; don't steal; don't commit adultery, etc.). Yet we often focus this commandment on our own children, forgetting that we, too, are children.

Think for a minute to whom this is written. This is a people wandering in the desert, looking for the Promised Land. Some minimal set of rules must govern a nomadic people journeying to an unknown place. And this makes the list. So let's examine what this might mean for us today. To do that, we must delve into the word that is translated "honor."

The Hebrew word for "honor" is *kabad*. It is used 113 times in the Old Testament, and it has the sense of something weighty. If something has weightiness in our lives, we assign value to it, but not just value—*high* value. Thus, to "honor" someone is to assign high value to that person in our lives.

The assignment of value is often cultural. Another good English synonym might be "esteem." In our culture, if you esteem someone, what do you do? What would make your father and mother feel esteemed by you as their child? What would make you feel esteemed by your own children? Think about that for a moment.

The biblical imperative to children is that we esteem our fathers and mothers—that we assign high value to them.

So what does that mean?

In my cultural reality, esteeming my parents would mean the following things practically:

- Asking for advice and implementing that advice (when appropriate)[1]
- Spending time with them
- Celebrating milestones with them
- Caring for them and helping bear burdens

In other cultures, assigning a high value and esteeming might look different, and you will need to work through what this looks like in your cultural reality.

While the way we assign value may be cultural in many respects, the urge to assign value to our parents is innate to some degree. I have worked with many children in the foster care system, and I can count on one hand how many of those children actually despise their biological parents. If given the opportunity, they would return to them in a heartbeat. It is only in cases of *serious* abuse that children completely detach from their parents.

God has placed this innate desire to honor our parents within the very fabric of our being, so it is highly likely that you will *know* if you are not honoring your parents. Unfortunately (or, perhaps, fortunately), the Bible does not include a twelve-step program that tells us exactly what it means to honor our parents. Nevertheless, it is extremely important that we let the Bible speak about the Bible. The New Testament can help us ascertain how this command should be interpreted and provide a more holistic view of what it means to honor.

In Ephesians 6:1–3, Paul expands on the Exodus passage and helps us understand a little better what is required:

> Children, obey your parents in the Lord, for this is right. "Honor your father and mother" (this is the first commandment with a promise), "that it may go well with you and that you may live long in the land."

In verses 2–3, Paul quotes the Exodus passage in full, so let's start there. The Greek word that Paul uses for "honor" in Ephesians 6:2 has an economic implication. This concept should be easy for us to grasp in our consumer culture.

I work as a product manager for a manufacturer of electrification products for transit and industrial applications. As a product manager, I am intricately involved in costing and pricing strategies for our product lines. What it costs to physically make something and what the consumer pays are two *vastly* different numbers.

One of the best questions that I have ever heard a manager ask a prospective employee during an interview is, "Let's say you're at the mall, and you see a pair of shoes on the shelf that you absolutely love. The shoes are $100. How much do you think it actually costs to make those shoes?" Generally, folks who have never been around manufacturing give answers in the $60–$70 range. Individuals who have been around manufacturing and supply chain management might guess between $35 and $50. In all likelihood, amidst the material, labor, and overhead, those shoes actually cost somewhere between $5 and $20 to make. Various middlemen, logistical concerns, and incentive structures are baked into that $100 price tag. Ultimately, though, that $100 price tag is assigned because you, as the consumer, have attributed that value to those shoes. That value is really about the argument that you have in your head about those shoes. And, like any good persuasive speech, that argument will be composed of at least one of three rhetorical devices: *pathos*, *logos*, and/or *ethos*.

Those shoes have a weightiness in your mind that may or may not actually exist. For most of us, that weightiness is not based on logic, but, rather, on emotion (*pathos*)—how those shoes will make us *feel*, how they will make us look, how we think they may perform in some activity in which we are involved, and how they might get us acceptance with the "in" crowd.

In some situations, that weightiness might actually be based on logic (*logos*). You might reason that if you were to craft a shoe, it would not come out looking anything like the item on the shelf before you and, even if it could, there is nothing you could do to actually make such a thing for much less than $1,000—by the time you buy all the material at market price, acquire any machines you might need to make it, and put in the inordinate amount of time to complete the project. Therefore, in your mind, those shoes are a bargain at $100! You have actually esteemed them at $1,000, so getting them for $100 just adds to the esteem you have for them.

Finally, in fewer situations, that weightiness is attributable to who else has the shoes (*ethos*). It could be the "in" crowd. It could be a celebrity or a respected individual in your life. You feel as though some of what you respect or esteem about the individual who supports those shoes might actually be attributed to you for wearing them. Thus, in addition to protecting your feet, they also have a weightiness worth $100 because of the value you place on the individual or group whom you see supporting them (this is why marketers use celebrity endorsements).

We can see this same concept at work in branding. At the time of this writing, a number of electronic brands command quite a bit of loyalty. Regardless of the industry, think about a product or brand on which you place a premium for whatever reason.

You value this product.
You value this brand.

This is honor, and you cannot be neutral about something that is honored.

It is talked about. It is held in high regard. You may hate that thing, or you may love that thing, but you feel that you have to defend that position. Ultimately, you assign a value based on your emotional (*pathos*), logical (*logos*), and/or personality (*ethos*) attachment to that product or brand.

We are to do the same thing with our father and mother.

We must attribute value to them. The Bible, in both the Old and New Testaments, tells us that we are to "honor" our parents. Wouldn't it be great if it fleshed that out a little for us? Like, "Here are ten ways to

> You cannot be neutral about something that is honored.

honor your parents in every season of life," but it does not. It does, however, give additional guidance for children who are still under their parents' authority, but it does not really tell us much about how we are to honor our fathers and our mothers as adults. Thus, we are left to seek the Holy Spirit's wisdom. If you have a minute, take some time right now to pray about how you might better honor your father and mother.

Obey

Remember how the previous chapter concluded by explaining that this chapter would help us to see the *how* and *why* we are to shift our dependence from parents to God? The first command that helps us with

that tactically is honor. Paul then takes that command from the Old Testament and expands on it in the New Testament.

But a bit of context is paramount.

The Ten Commandments in Exodus 20 were for all the people of Israel. It is not as though "honor your father and mother" was written to those who were younger in age, whereas the other nine commandments were for adults. No. These commandments were for everyone.

However, in this Ephesians passage, Paul is specifically dealing with roles in Christian households. In chapter 5, he addresses husbands and wives and, in chapter 6, he addresses children and parents. So in this section of Scripture, these children *are* children who are young in age. Thus, for children who are younger in age, Paul adds, "obey." "Children, *obey* your parents in the Lord, for this is right" (Ephesians 6:1, emphasis mine).

Paul begins his instruction to children in Ephesians 6:1 by saying that children are to "obey" their parents, and he qualifies the first sentence by quoting the command from Exodus 20. Whatever Paul means by "obey," then, it is safe to assume that, at a minimum, this obedience requires "honor." We have already considered what "honor" means. Let us now consider what "obey" means?

The Greek word used for "obey" in the Ephesians passage is *hupakouō*. The first portion of this word, *hupa*, literally means "under." Think of the term hypodermic needle (*hypo*, meaning "under"; *dermis*, meaning "skin"). So in this situation, we have *hupa* meaning "under" and *akouō* meaning "to hear" (think "acoustic"). Therefore, *hupakouō*, could literally be translated as "under the hearing [of someone]." What is important, particularly for later in this book, is distinguishing between *hupakouō* (to obey) and *hupotassō* (to submit). *Hupotassō* is the word used in the previous chapter to refer to Jesus' relationship with His parents as He began shifting His dependences from obedience to honor—and it is a word we will explore more in-depth when we discuss "submission" in the chapters on marriage.

Twenty-one verses in the New Testament employ this word for "obedience" (*hupakouō*). If you read through all of them in one sitting, the sense you are left with is that, in many instances, the object or individual obeying is in some way bound to obedience through either natural or legal order. This is quite a different sense than when you read through the verses about "submission" (*hupotassō*).

Children are to *hupakouō* (obey) their parents. Simply put, children are to do what their parents say because parents are the natural authority of children.

In the previous section on honor, I talked about my experience with children in the foster care system. I mentioned how so few of those children actually despise their parents—how valuing our parents is innate.

This is part of God's design.

Parents are the natural authority of the child, and children, consequently, are under the natural authority of their parents.

Now, thinking about my own children's behavior, that may seem rather hard to believe, but perhaps I can illustrate using an example from my own childhood. When I was growing up, we had a rule in our house—no R-rated movies. Period. We did not discuss whether the movie had redeeming qualities. I can remember trying to argue about this when I was in high school, and many of my friends were going to see *Braveheart* and *Saving Private Ryan*. I mean, some churches were even using these films in sermon illustrations!

To no avail.

No R-rated movies.

Period.

I watched my first R-rated movie when I was in college, and I can remember the guilt that I felt. The guilt did not concern any movie content. No, my guilt came from the knowledge that I had done something that I knew would displease my parents.

As children, this is what obedience and honor get us. They get us a healthy sense of guilt when we have violated the rules of our parents. This is called conviction when we feel it as children of God.

However, the obedience in Scripture is slightly more nuanced than the simple definition of "do what you're told." We have already seen that the obedience found in Scripture includes honor, and honor deals with the heart. It is possible to obey from a wrong motive, just as the older brother exhibited in the story of the prodigal son. He was dutiful, yet his heart was far from the father. Thus, in Ephesians, Paul tells children to obey their parents and follows up with, "Honor your father and mother." This changes the focus of the obedience. Children are to do what their parents tell them—not only because they are under the natural authority of their parent, but also because that obedience should flow from a heart of honor. And a heart of honor is, ultimately, a heart that wants to please the Lord by esteeming parents.

So when does obedience end?

Well, the only clear scriptural cutoff is marriage: "Therefore a man shall leave his father and his mother and hold fast to his wife, and they shall become one flesh" (Genesis 2:24). There are a lot of Christian thinkers who would extrapolate this to include when a child leaves the household and essentially forms his or her own family unit. And this makes sense when we reflect upon what we have already discovered about this topic.

First, childhood is not a journey to independence, but, rather, a journey to shift dependence from earthly parents to our heavenly Father. In that scenario, when children have the autonomy and ability to choose God or self for themselves, then the emphasis shifts from *obedience* to their parents to *honoring* their father and mother.

Second, when we consider that part of the definition of obedience is being under the natural or *legal* authority of the parent, it follows that that authority ends at some point. The legal sense is going to differ from country to country, and the natural sense is becoming increasingly important because children are being given more and more leverage to make potentially damaging decisions as "rights." From a natural sense, then, when children can operate on their own—when they can function outside of the authority of their family unit (both legally and naturally)—then they no longer have to obey; albeit, they are still required to honor. But again, it is about the heart. Ultimately, neither obedience nor honor can be forced.[2]

Since we have just examined the roots of these two words—"honor" and "obey"—I do want to say something briefly to parents.

To some degree, it is incumbent on parents to give their children enough rope to allow them cultural flexibility (i.e., to not exasperate them—see Ephesians 6:4).

At the end of the day, the parent is the designated authority of the child. The parent is responsible for setting the rules. Additionally, it is incumbent upon the parent to reflect upon the rules and principles that govern their homes. Are they done for biblical reasons, or are they just an extension of pride so that your child doesn't embarrass you? These things are often deep-rooted heart issues that take years to discover. But more on that later, when we get to parenting.

Learn

This is the final section, and it is short. It is short because, to some extent, it is a subtopic of obedience; however, I think enough biblical evidence exists for me to include it. Let me tell you the reason.

First of all, children are to obey their parents. Scripturally, parents are to teach their children. Consequently, if children are to obey their parents, and parents are to teach their children, it follows that children are to learn what they are being taught.

Second, children are told numerous times in Scripture to "listen" and "obey." Much of the book of Proverbs encourages children to "hear" or "forsake not" the teachings of their parents. Hence, it is incumbent upon children to take in the teaching they are being given. This is closely related to being obedient (and therefore learning) what you are being taught. But, as with obedience, there is a slight twist. In these proverbs, the child is actually commanded to hear and obey. Yet learning involves one level beyond simply hearing and obeying. It is about the heart. You can obey and disagree. Learning involves internalizing what is being taught. It is incumbent upon children to hear and obey what is being taught, but if they do not internalize it, they have not really learned it. The best way to hear and obey is through internalizing and making it one's own. Let me illustrate with a story.

This past week, we became pet people. Both my wife and I had pets when we were children, and we both had good experiences. Neither of us, however, really had a strong desire for a pet when we got married. Our daughter, who is six years old, began asking for a pet about a year ago. We put it off as long as we could, using the responsibility card (i.e., you have to prove that you are responsible enough to own a pet). Then we told her she could have a pet when we got back from vacation. This year has been a busy year with a lot of travel for our family, so we waited until the last trip to tell her she could get a pet.

She settled on a guinea pig.

So on a cold January afternoon, we all piled into the car and headed for the pet store. I had already prepared her that the pet store might not have guinea pigs that day, and that we really needed to set up the guinea pig's cage before we brought it home. When we arrived at the pet store, we started looking at the cages and all the accessories. It wasn't long before an employee came over and began helping us by asking questions and providing care tips for guinea pigs. When I asked whether they actually had any guinea pigs, she informed me that they did not, but they should be getting some early the next week.

She asked if we wanted her to call her sister, who worked at the pet store across town. I told her that would be fine. Her sister informed us

that they had *one* guinea pig left, and asked if we wanted her to hold it for us. One look into my daughter's eyes after a yearlong wait answered that question. I told her to hold it for us, and we all piled in the car and drove across town to the next pet store. When we arrived, the sister of the helper from the first store looked a bit distraught. She apologetically informed us that someone had bought the guinea pig before she could set it aside. By the time she called her sister back to tell her, we had already left the first store.

There were some tears, but I was quite proud of my daughter. She did not cry for long. This experience taught her delayed gratification. After waiting for so long to obtain a pet, she was being told that it would still be a little longer. This was a huge disappointment, but one she probably needed, particularly since she is growing up in a time when she has immediate access to just about any information. She can get nearly any product that she wants—if not immediately, then within two days, using subscribed shipping.

My wife looked at me during the heightened emotion of this event and mouthed the name of yet another pet store in the area. Thankfully, the helper at the store saw this interaction and shook her head to inform us that not even her competitor had guinea pigs because of the Christmas rush. When we got in the car, I told my wife that she had almost been "that mom." Her poor little baby was sad about something, so we were going to fix it at whatever cost. The extra few days of anticipation did Sophie a world of good. She appreciated the guinea pig that much more when she finally got it.

That was a good lesson.

Today, though, was the first time that her appreciation was tested. Today my daughter had to clean out her new pet's cage.

The guinea pig's name is Acorn—Acorn Giggles.

Here is what I noticed.

My daughter was focused.

More focused than I was.

In fact, it took everything in me to not just do the task for her. It would have been *so* much faster (talk about being affected by—and reinforcing—instant gratification). I had things to do (like writing this story). However, when I simply gave her a task and walked away, although it took her ten times longer than it would have taken me, she did the task out of joy and out of love for little Acorn. She also did it thoroughly.

I almost took that away from her due to my impatience.

It took nearly an hour for her to clean the cage and then another hour for her to dry the cage. Yet, by letting her do it, I was teaching her not just how to clean and dry something, but also how to take responsibility. This story illustrates two forms of learning that children (both young and old) need to be doing.

The first form is learning from life's lessons, and this type of learning is circumstantial. Like my daughter having to learn patience when the store did not have a guinea pig, many times God sends circumstances into His children's lives in order that we learn something. Perhaps we have become too selfish. Perhaps we have idolized something. Perhaps we have become too dependent upon ourselves. God may use life circumstances to highlight these aspects of our lives even though—in the moment—those lessons might be painful.

The second form of learning that children need is the development of new skill sets. Ultimately, we work as unto the Lord (Colossians 3:23), so we need to let the love and joy of serving the Lord dwell in us as we perform the duties and expand the responsibilities He has given us (while simultaneously not *neglecting* our other responsibilities). For me, this has actually meant limiting some of my career responsibilities to concentrate on some of my responsibilities at home. And, as I mentioned in the story above, the skill set I needed to learn on cage-cleaning day was patience.

The primary reason to include learning as a necessity for children is, ultimately, because of the very premise of this book. The premise is that God created these relationships to reflect how we are to interact with Him. It is clear from Scripture that, as children of God, we are to learn. And that is a great segue into the next chapter, where we will explore how the truths found in the physical relationship of being a child mirror our relationship with God.

www.ingramcontent.com/pod-product-compliance
Lightning Source LLC
Chambersburg PA
CBHW061154010526
44118CB00027B/2969